States

KANSAS

by Angie Swanson

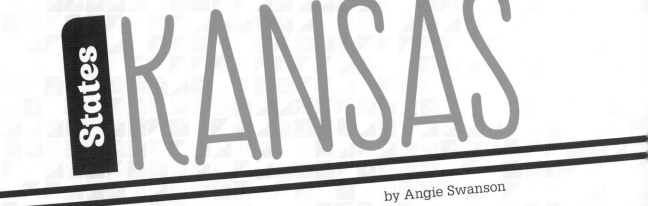

CAPSTONE PRESS
a capstone imprint

Next Page Books are published by Capstone Press,
1710 Roe Crest Drive, North Mankato, Minnesota 56003
www.mycapstone.com

Library of Congress Cataloging-in-Publication Data
Cataloging-in-publication information is on file with the Library of
Congress.
ISBN 978-1-5157-0403-4 (library binding)
ISBN 978-1-5157-0462-1 (paperback)
ISBN 978-1-5157-0514-7 (ebook PDF)

Editorial Credits
Jaclyn Jaycox, editor; Richard Korab and Katy LaVigne, designers;
Morgan Walters, media researcher; Laura Manthe, production specialist

Photo Credits
Alamy: Florilegius, 25, Stephen Saks Photography, 9; Capstone Press:
Angi Gahler, map 4, 7; CriaImages.com: Jay Robert Nash Collection,
12, top 19; Dreamstime: Karen Hoar, 17; Getty Images: Ed Zurga, 16,
Kansas City Star, 27; Library of Congress: Prints and Photographs
Division Washington, D.C., top 18, middle 18, bottom 18, New York
Times, New York, U.S.A., 28; North Wind Picture Archives, 26; One
Mile Up, Inc., flag, seal 23; Shutterstock: Action Sports Photography,
13, Aliaksei Smalenski, bottom 24, Cartela, top left 20, Daniel Prudek,
bottom right 20, DFree, middle 19, El Nariz, 15, eukukulka, 14,
Featureflash, bottom 19, Fredlyfish4, 6, Henryk Sadura, 5, Jason
Patrick Ross, top left 21, Kanjanee Chaisin, top 24, Matt Jeppson,
middle right 21, max voran, bottom left 8, top right 20, Michael
Vorobiev, 7, Ricardo Reitmeyer, cover, 11, Rusty Dodson, 10, science
photo, middle left 21, Steve Byland, top right 21, Tom Reichner, bottom
left 20, Weldon Schloneger, bottom right 8; United States Department of
Agriculture, bottom 21; Wikimedia: FEMA Photo Library, 29

All design elements by Shutterstock

Printed and bound in China.
0316/CA21600187
012016   009436F16

TABLE OF CONTENTS

LOCATION..4

GEOGRAPHY 6

WEATHER..8

LANDMARKS...9

HISTORY AND GOVERNMENT................12

INDUSTRY 14

POPULATION...16

FAMOUS PEOPLE.....................................18

STATE SYMBOLS......................................20

FAST FACTS..22

KANSAS TIMELINE..................................25

Glossary 30

Read More 31

Internet Sites 31

Critical Thinking Using the Common Core 32

Index 32

Want to take your research further? Ask your librarian if your school subscribes to PebbleGo Next. If so, when you see this helpful symbol 🖱 throughout the book, log onto www.pebblegonext.com for bonus downloads and information.

LOCATION

Kansas is located in the center of the connected 48 states. Kansas lies between Nebraska, which is to the north, and Oklahoma, which is to the south. To the east is Missouri, and to the west is Colorado. The Missouri River makes a jagged notch along Kansas' northeast border. Topeka, the state capital, lies along the Kansas River. Wichita, Overland Park, and Kansas City are the largest cities in Kansas.

PebbleGo Next Bonus!
To print and label your own map, go to www.pebblegonext.com and search keywords:
KS MAP

N
W E
S

NEBRASKA

Missouri River

COLORADO

Oakley •

Minneapolis •

Manhattan •
Topeka ✪

Kansas City •

• Salina

Lawrence •

Overland Park •

KANSAS

Garden City •

Hutchinson •

Dodge City •

Wichita •

MISSOURI

OKLAHOMA

Legend
✪ Capital
• City
⌇ River

Scale
Miles
0   25   50   75   100
0   25   50   75   100
Kilometers

Wichita is located on the Arkansas River and is home to 386,552 people.

GEOGRAPHY

Kansas is divided into three main regions. They are the Great Plains, Dissected Till Plains, and Southeastern Plains. The Great Plains spread across central and western Kansas. The western part of the Great Plains contains the state's highest point. Mount Sunflower rises 4,039 feet (1,231 meters) above sea level. The Dissected Till Plains are in the state's northeastern corner. The Big Blue River forms this region's western border. The Southeastern Plains is east of the Great Plains and south of the Dissected Till Plains.

PebbleGo Next Bonus! To watch a video about fossils found in Kansas, go to www.pebblegonext.com and search keywords: **KS VIDEO**

Visitors may see antelope, deer, prairie dogs, and other wildlife on Mount Sunflower.

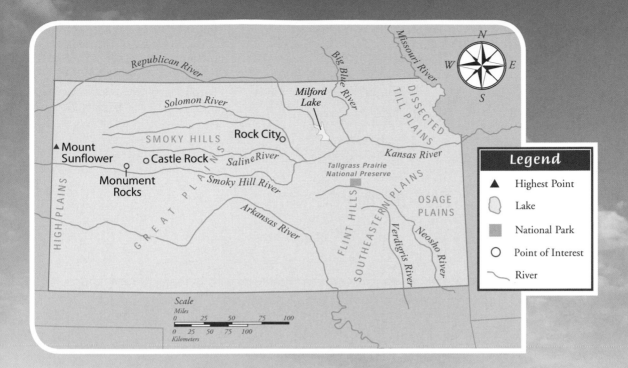

Also known as the "Wheat State,"
Kansas has more than 46 million acres
(19 million hectares) of farmland.

WEATHER

Kansas' weather changes widely between the seasons. Winter is cold and windy, while summer is hot and sunny. The average winter temperature is 30 degrees Fahrenheit (minus 1 degree Celsius). The average summer temperature is 77°F (25°C).

Average High and Low Temperatures (Topeka, KS)

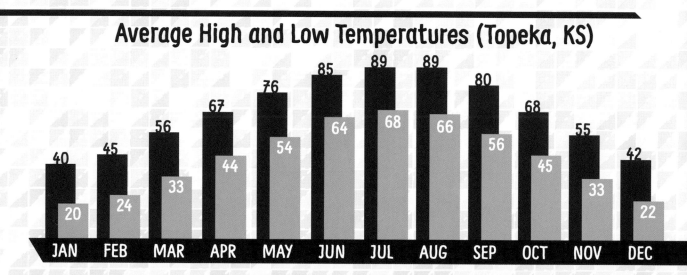

	JAN	FEB	MAR	APR	MAY	JUN	JUL	AUG	SEP	OCT	NOV	DEC
High	40	45	56	67	76	85	89	89	80	68	55	42
Low	20	24	33	44	54	64	68	66	56	45	33	22

Land of Oz Museum

In Liberal, people can visit the Land of Oz Museum. It features objects from the movie *The Wizard of Oz*, which made Kansas famous. Liberal has a paved yellow brick road inspired from the movie. Each October the town hosts a festival called Oztoberfest.

Monument Rocks

Monument Rocks near Oakley rises 70 feet (21 m) above the plains. The formations, also called the Chalk Pyramids, formed about 80 million years ago. Visitors can view forms that look like towers, arches, and keyholes.

Tallgrass Prairie National Preserve

Near the Flint Hills, Tallgrass Prairie National Preserve protects thousands of acres of native grasslands. It's the largest stretch of tallgrass prairie remaining in North America.

HISTORY AND GOVERNMENT

Wichita became a major railway intersection by 1875. The city became known as one of the wildest towns in the West.

In the 1500s several American Indian tribes lived in Kansas. In 1541 Francisco Vásquez de Coronado led Spanish explorers from Mexico to Kansas. French explorers arrived in the 1600s. France claimed a large area in 1682. This area, which included present-day Kansas, was called Louisiana. In 1803 President Thomas Jefferson bought Louisiana from France in the Louisiana Purchase. In 1830 Congress passed the Indian Removal Act, requiring American Indian tribes to move to Kansas and other lands west of the Mississippi River. The Territory of Kansas was established in 1854, allowing people to settle in the territory. In 1861 Kansas became the 34th U.S. state.

Kansas' government is divided into three branches. The governor is the leader of the executive branch. The legislature is made up of the 125-member House of Representatives and the 40-member Senate. Judges and their courts make up the judicial branch. They uphold the laws.

Kansas' capitol building is located in Topeka.

INDUSTRY

Kansas' economy depends on agriculture, manufacturing, and service industries. Farmland covers about 90 percent of Kansas' land. Kansas leads the nation in wheat production. It is also a top producer of grain sorghum. Many farmers in Kansas raise beef cattle. Farmers also grow corn, soybeans, and sunflowers.

Kansas leads the nation in manufacturing aircraft. Manufacturers with plants in Wichita include Boeing, Cessna, Raytheon, and Bombardier. Several aircraft research companies are located in Kansas. Food processing is another important Kansas industry. Meatpacking plants process beef. Mills grind wheat into flour.

Kansas grows enough wheat each year to bake 36 billion loaves of bread.

Most jobs in Kansas are in service industries. Government workers, teachers, retail clerks, bankers, and insurance agents are all service workers.

Kansas has a diverse mix of industries, including food processing and meatpacking.

POPULATION

Kansans have many ethnic backgrounds. Most Kansans descended from European immigrants. These people came to the United States in the 1800s from Germany, Russia, England, France, Sweden, and other European countries. More than 2 million white people now live in Kansas. During the early 1900s, many people moved to Kansas from Mexico. The state's Hispanic population is now about 300,000. More than 160,000 African-Americans and about 67,000 Asians also live in Kansas. About 23,000 American Indians are Kansans. Members of the Potawatomi, Iowa, Sac and Fox, and Kickapoo tribes reside in the state.

Population by Ethnicity

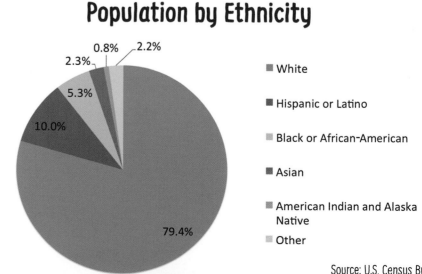

- 0.8%
- 2.2%
- 2.3%
- 5.3%
- 10.0%
- 79.4%

- White
- Hispanic or Latino
- Black or African-American
- Asian
- American Indian and Alaska Native
- Other

Source: U.S. Census Bureau.

FAMOUS PEOPLE

Charles Curtis (1860–1936) was the first person of American Indian ancestry to serve as U.S. vice president (1929–1933). He was born in Topeka.

Amelia Earhart (1897–1937) was the first woman to fly solo across the Atlantic Ocean in 1932. She was born in Atchison.

Dwight D. Eisenhower (1890–1969) was the 34th U.S. president (1953–1961). Born in Texas, he grew up in Abilene.

Gwendolyn Brooks (1917–2000) was the first African-American to win a Pulitzer Prize. She won it for her poetry collection *Annie Allen* (1949). She was born in Topeka.

Kirstie Alley (1955–) is an actress. She became famous for her role in the TV series *Cheers*. She was born in Wichita.

Jeff Probst (1961–) is a TV personality and the award-winning host of the TV show *Survivor*. He was born in Wichita.

STATE SYMBOLS

Tree

cottonwood

Flower

native sunflower

Bird

western meadowlark

Insect

honeybee

PebbleGo Next Bonus! To make a dessert using produce from Kansas, go to www.pebblegonext.com and search keywords: **KS RECIPE**

Reptile

ornate box turtle

Animal

American buffalo (bison)

Soil

harney silt loam

Amphibian

barred tiger salamander

Grass

little bluestem

FAST FACTS

STATEHOOD
1861

CAPITAL ☆
Topeka

LARGEST CITY •
Wichita

SIZE
81,759 square miles (211,755 square kilometers) land area (2010 U.S. Census Bureau)

POPULATION
2,893,957 (2013 U.S. Census estimate)

STATE NICKNAME
Sunflower State

STATE MOTTO
"Ad astra per aspera," which is Latin for "To the stars through difficulties"

STATE SEAL

The state seal shows many symbols of nature, history, and industry in Kansas. The sun rising over a mountain represents the east, where most of Kansas' early settlers came from. A steamboat on a river represents trade. A settler's cabin and a man plowing in a field stand for Kansas' agriculture. A line of covered wagons stands for pioneers' westward journey. American Indians pursue a herd of buffalo, representing Kansas' past as an American Indian homeland. At the top of the seal is the state motto. "Ad astra per aspera" means "To the stars through difficulties." Beneath it, a cluster of 34 stars stands for Kansas' place as the 34th state.

STATE FLAG

PebbleGo Next Bonus!
To print and color your own flag, go to www.pebblegonext.com and search keywords:
KS FLAG

The Kansas state flag is royal blue, with the state's name at the bottom and the state seal in the center. Above the seal, a sunflower represents Kansas' nickname, the Sunflower State. The Kansas state seal includes a rising sun, a farmer plowing a field, and wagons heading west. Other images on the seal are a herd of buffalo, two American Indians, and a steamboat traveling on a river. The state motto is at the top of the seal. Underneath the motto, 34 stars represent Kansas' position as the 34th state.

MINING PRODUCTS

petroleum, natural gas, helium, salt

MANUFACTURED GOODS

transportation equipment, food products, petroleum, chemicals, machinery, computer and electronic products

FARM PRODUCTS

wheat, sorghum, corn, hay, soybeans, sunflowers, cattle, sheep

KANSAS TIMELINE

1500s Kansa, Pawnee, Osage, and Wichita people are living in present-day Kansas when European explorers arrive.

1541 Spanish explorer Francisco Vásquez de Coronado crosses present-day Kansas.

1620 The Pilgrims establish a colony in the New World in present-day Massachusetts.

1682 French explorer René-Robert Cavelier, known as Sieur de La Salle, claims the Mississippi Valley, including Kansas, for France.

 **1803** The United States buys a large area of land from France, including present-day Kansas. The sale is called the Louisiana Purchase.

1804–1819 American explorers Meriwether Lewis, William Clark, Zebulon Pike, and Stephen Long travel through Kansas.

 **1854** The Territory of Kansas is established.

 **1861** Kansas becomes the 34th state on January 29.

1861–1865

The Union and the Confederacy fight the Civil War. Kansas fights for the Union. Nearly 8,500 Kansan soldiers die in the Civil War.

1887

Susanna Salter is elected mayor of Argonia, Kansas, becoming the first woman mayor in the country.

1914–1918

World War I is fought; the United States enters the war in 1917.

1931–1938

Kansas and much of the Midwest experience a severe drought; the area is called the Dust Bowl.

**1939–1945** World War II is fought; the United States enters the war in 1941.

**1952** Kansas native Dwight D. Eisenhower is elected the 34th president.

**1972** The Soviet Union loses crops due to a drought. Much of Kansas' wheat crop is part of a large sale to the Soviet Union.

1991 Joan Finney becomes Kansas' first female governor.

**2002**

A bronze statue of an American Indian warrior is mounted atop the capitol building in Topeka. This officially completes the building more than 100 years after its construction.

**2007**

A tornado hits Greenburg on May 7, killing 11 people and destroying nearly 1,000 homes and businesses.

2011

On January 29 Kansas marks 150 years of statehood with its annual Kansas Day celebration.

2015

A cyclist from Lawrence breaks the speed record for crossing Kansas from west to east; the final time is 23 hours and 53 minutes.

Glossary

ancestry *(AN-sess-tree)*—members of your family who lived long ago, usually before your grandparents

descend *(di-SEND)*—to belong to a later generation of the same family

ethnicity *(ETH-niss-ih-tee)*—a group of people who share the same physical features, beliefs, and backgrounds

executive *(ig-ZE-kyuh-tiv)*—the branch of government that makes sure laws are followed

immigrant *(IM-uh-gruhnt)*—a person who leaves one country and settles in another

industry *(IN-duh-stree)*—a business which produces a product or provides a service

legislature *(LEJ-iss-lay-chur)*—a group of elected officials who have the power to make or change laws for a country or state

petroleum *(puh-TROH-lee-uhm)*—an oily liquid found below the earth's surface used to make gasoline, heating oil, and many other products

region *(REE-juhn)*—a large area

sea level *(SEE LEV-uhl)*—the average level of the surface of the ocean, used as a starting point from which to measure the height or depth of any place

Read More

Bailer, Darice. *What's Great About Kansas?* Our Great States. Minneapolis: Lerner Publications, 2016.

Ganeri, Anita. *United States of America: A Benjamin Blog and His Inquisitive Dog Guide.* Country Guides. Chicago: Heinemann Raintree, 2015.

King, David C. *Kansas.* It's My State! New York: Cavendish Square Pub., 2016.

Internet Sites

FactHound offers a safe, fun way to find Internet sites related to this book. All of the sites on FactHound have been researched by our staff.

Here's all you do:

Visit *www.facthound.com*

Type in this code: 9781515704034

 Check out projects, games and lots more at
www.capstonekids.com

Critical Thinking Using the Common Core

1. What happened to Kansas in the year 1854? (Key Ideas and Details)

2. Tallgrass Prairie National Preserve protects thousands of acres of native grasslands in Kansas. Why is it important to protect grasslands and other natural areas? (Integration of Knowledge and Ideas)

3. Look at the graph on page 8. On average, what's the coldest month in Topeka? (Craft and Structure)

Index

American Indians, 12, 16, 23, 25, 29

capital, 4, 18, 22

economy, 14–15

ethnicities, 16

famous people, 18–19

farming, 14, 24

government, 12, 13, 18, 27, 28

history, 12, 25–29

landmarks, 9–11
    Land of Oz Museum, 9
    Monument Rocks, 10
    Tallgrass Prairie National Preserve, 11

manufacturing, 14, 24

mining, 24

population, 16, 22

size, 22

state symbols, 20–21, 23

weather, 8, 27, 29